Discard

Little People, BIG DREAMS

JEAN-MICHEL BASQUIAT

Written by
Maria Isabel Sánchez Vegara

Illustrated by
Luciano Lozano

Frances Lincoln
Children's Books

Jean-Michel was a talented boy from Brooklyn whose mother was Puerto Rican and father was Haitian. He was only four when he started drawing, eager to show the world what a great artist he could be.

For Jean-Michel, a perfect Saturday was going to Manhattan with his mother to visit its wonderful museums. Back home, he spent all afternoon drawing cartoons on scrap paper while listening to music with his father.

One day, when he was seven, Jean-Michel was hit by a car while playing in the street. He had to rest in bed for weeks. To help pass the time, his mother gave him the most useful present he could have received: an anatomy book.

Skulls, teeth, guts, skins, skeletons...the book was simply fascinating! Going through its pages, Jean-Michel realized how powerful and fragile the human body is. He decided to use all he had learned in his paintings.

Things turned upside down when his mother got ill. Jean-Michel dropped out of school and ran away from home. Luckily, he found his place in City-As-School, an unconventional setting where he met other artists like him.

Not long afterward, the city of New York woke up with messages spray-painted on buildings all over Manhattan. They were signed with a name that Jean-Michel and his friend Ad Diaz had made up: SAMO.

It was the beginning of the graffiti era, and Jean-Michel was at the center of it. In the blink of an eye, he went from selling T-shirts and homemade postcards, to becoming the new star of the art scene.

Locked up in his studio, Jean-Michel spent hours on the floor, mixing pencil, oil sticks, and crayons with cut-up quotes he found in comics and history books. The result was a beautiful mess of paintings that people fell in love with.

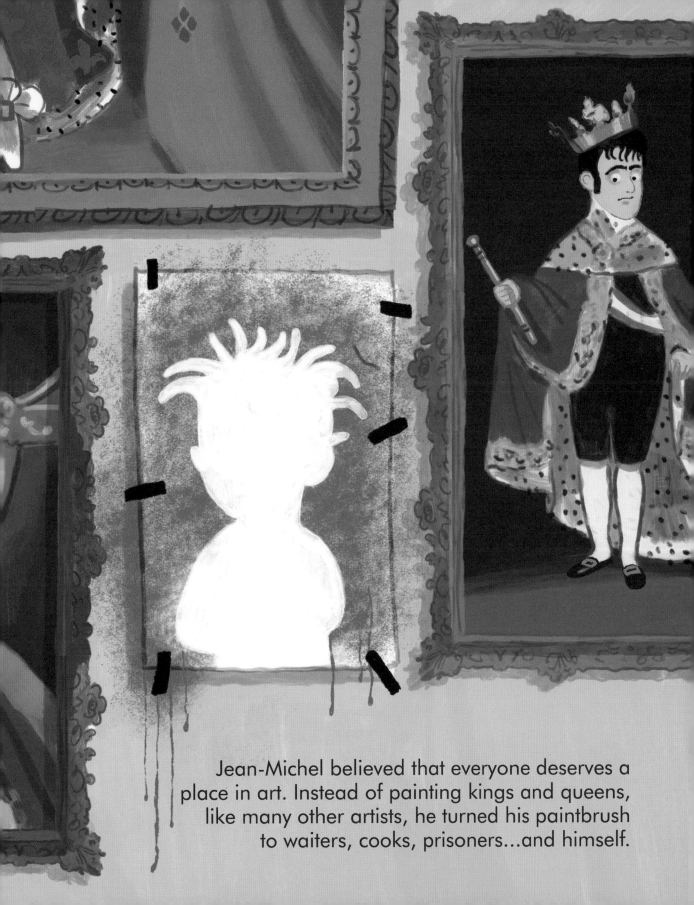

Jean-Michel believed that everyone deserves a place in art. Instead of painting kings and queens, like many other artists, he turned his paintbrush to waiters, cooks, prisoners...and himself.

If there was someone he wanted to meet, it was the famous Andy Warhol, one of his idols. After their first lunch, Jean-Michel went home and within two hours he sent Andy a wet painting of the two of them.

It was the beginning of a great friendship! Jean-Michel and Andy spent lots of time together: working, painting and going to parties. They were the brand-new painter and pop art legend—the craziest pair on the scene!

In less than ten years, Jean-Michel made thousands of paintings and drawings. But he was also a poet, a musician, and a graffiti prodigy who influenced the work of many artists that came after him.

And by painting life in his own unique way, Jean-Michel became one of the most important artists of the 20th century. The talented child who once told his father: "Papa, I'm going to be famous."

JEAN-MICHEL BASQUIAT

(Born 1960 – Died 1988)

c. 1970s   c.1970s

Jean-Michel Basquiat was born in Brooklyn, New York, as the second
of four children to Matilde and Gerard Basquiat. His older brother,
Max, died before his arrival but he had two younger sisters: Lisane and
Jeanine. His mother, Matilde, was a key source of encouragement to
her bright, young son, who had learned to read, write, and draw by the
age of four. His copy of *Gray's Anatomy*, which Matilde gave him as he
recovered from a car accident, sparked a keen interest in the human
form. Jean-Michel's parents divorced when he was a teenager, and he
went to live with his father after his mother was admitted to a mental
institution. He fought with his father and left home at age 17, supporting
himself by selling T-shirts and homemade postcards. Around that time,

c.1985

1988

he moved his canvas to the street, painting late at night on buildings in New York's East Village. Although he lacked formal training, Jean-Michel understood the power of combining image and word, and used his art to express the things around him, from high culture to jazz. Able to reduce his subject matter to its basic form, his portraits spoke boldly about racism and social inequality. His first painting sold for $25,000, propelling him to fame, and he gathered friends, including Andy Warhol, with whom he collaborated on 25 shows. Jean-Michel revolutionized the art world and changed perceptions on what art could be: a "springboard for deeper truths" as he once described it. Although he died young, his work is the greatest single influence on street art culture around the world today.

Want to find out more about **Jean-Michel Basquiat?**

Read one of these great books:

Life Doesn't Frighten Me by Maya Angelou and Jean-Michel Basquiat

Radiant Child by Javaka Steptoe

Brimming with creative inspiration, how-to projects, and useful information to enrich your everyday life, Quarto Knows is a favorite destination for those pursuing their interests and passions. Visit our site and dig deeper with our books into your area of interest: Quarto Creates, Quarto Cooks, Quarto Homes, Quarto Lives, Quarto Drives, Quarto Explores, Quarto Gifts, or Quarto Kids.

Concept and text © 2020 Maria Isabel Sánchez Vegara. Illustrations © 2020 Luciano Lozano.

First Published in the UK in 2020 by Frances Lincoln Children's Books, an imprint of The Quarto Group.

400 First Avenue North, Suite 400, Minneapolis, MN 55401, USA.

T (612) 344-8100 F (612) 344-8692 **www.QuartoKnows.com**

First Published in Spain in 2020 under the title Pequeño & Grande Jean-Michel Basquiat

by Alba Editorial, s.l.u., Baixada de Sant Miquel, 1, 08002 Barcelona

www.albaeditorial.es

All rights reserved.

Published by arrangement with Alba Editorial, s.l.u. Translation rights arranged by IMC Agència Literària, SL

All rights reserved.

A catalog record for this book is available from the British Library.

ISBN 978-0-7112-4580-8

Set in Futura BT.

Published by Katie Cotton • Designed by Karissa Santos

Edited by Rachel Williams and Katy Flint • Production by Caragh McAleenan

Manufactured in Guangdong, China CC032020

1 3 5 7 9 8 4 6 2

Photographic acknowledgements (pages 28-29, from left to right) 1. From Boom For Real: The Late Teenage Years of Jean-Michel Basquiat, 2017 © TCD/Prod.DB/Alexis Adler via Alamy Stock Photo 2. Boom For Real: The Late Teenage Years of Jean-Michel Basquiat, 2017 © TCD/Prod.DB via Alamy Stock Photo 3. American artist Jean-Michel Basquiat (1960 - 1988), c. 1985 © Rose Hartman via Getty Images 4. American artist, musician and producer of Haitian and Puerto Rican origins Jean-Michel Basquiat, in front of one of his paintings, during an exhibition at the Yvon Lambert gallery, 1988 © Julio Donoso/Sygma via Getty Images

Collect the
Little People, **BIG DREAMS** series:

FRIDA KAHLO

ISBN: 978-1-84780-783-0

COCO CHANEL

ISBN: 978-1-84780-784-7

MAYA ANGELOU

ISBN: 978-1-84780-889-9

AMELIA EARHART

ISBN: 978-1-84780-888-2

AGATHA CHRISTIE

ISBN: 978-1-84780-960-5

MARIE CURIE

ISBN: 978-1-84780-962-9

ROSA PARKS

ISBN: 978-1-78603-018-4

AUDREY HEPBURN

ISBN: 978-1-78603-053-5

EMMELINE PANKHURST

ISBN: 978-1-78603-020-7

ELLA FITZGERALD

ISBN: 978-1-78603-087-0

ADA LOVELACE

ISBN: 978-1-78603-076-4

JANE AUSTEN

ISBN: 978-1-78603-120-4

GEORGIA O'KEEFFE

ISBN: 978-1-78603-122-8

HARRIET TUBMAN

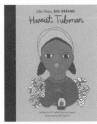

ISBN: 978-1-78603-227-0

ANNE FRANK

ISBN: 978-1-78603-229-4

MOTHER TERESA

ISBN: 978-1-78603-230-0

JOSEPHINE BAKER

ISBN: 978-1-78603-228-7

L. M. MONTGOMERY

ISBN: 978-1-78603-233-1

JANE GOODALL

ISBN: 978-1-78603-231-7

SIMONE DE BEAUVOIR

ISBN: 978-1-78603-232-4

MUHAMMAD ALI

ISBN: 978-1-78603-331-4

STEPHEN HAWKING

ISBN: 978-1-78603-333-8

MARIA MONTESSORI

ISBN: 978-1-78603-755-8

VIVIENNE WESTWOOD

ISBN: 978-1-78603-757-2

MAHATMA GANDHI

ISBN: 978-1-78603-787-9

DAVID BOWIE

ISBN: 978-1-78603-332-1

WILMA RUDOLPH

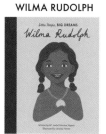

ISBN: 978-1-78603-751-0

DOLLY PARTON

ISBN: 978-1-78603-760-2

BRUCE LEE

ISBN: 978-1-78603-789-3

RUDOLF NUREYEV

ISBN: 978-1-78603-791-6

ZAHA HADID

ISBN: 978-1-78603-745-9

MARY SHELLEY

ISBN: 978-1-78603-748-0

MARTIN LUTHER KING JR.

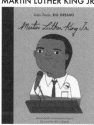

ISBN: 978-0-7112-4567-9

DAVID ATTENBOROUGH

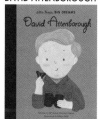

ISBN: 978-0-7112-4564-8

ASTRID LINDGREN

ISBN: 978-0-7112-5217-2

EVONNE GOOLAGONG

ISBN: 978-0-7112-4586-0

BOB DYLAN

ISBN: 978-0-7112-4675-1

ALAN TURING

ISBN: 978-0-7112-4678-2

BILLIE JEAN KING

ISBN: 978-0-7112-4693-5

GRETA THUNBERG

ISBN: 978-0-7112-5645-3

JESSE OWENS

ISBN: 978-0-7112-4583-9

JEAN-MICHEL BASQUIAT

ISBN: 978-0-7112-4580-8

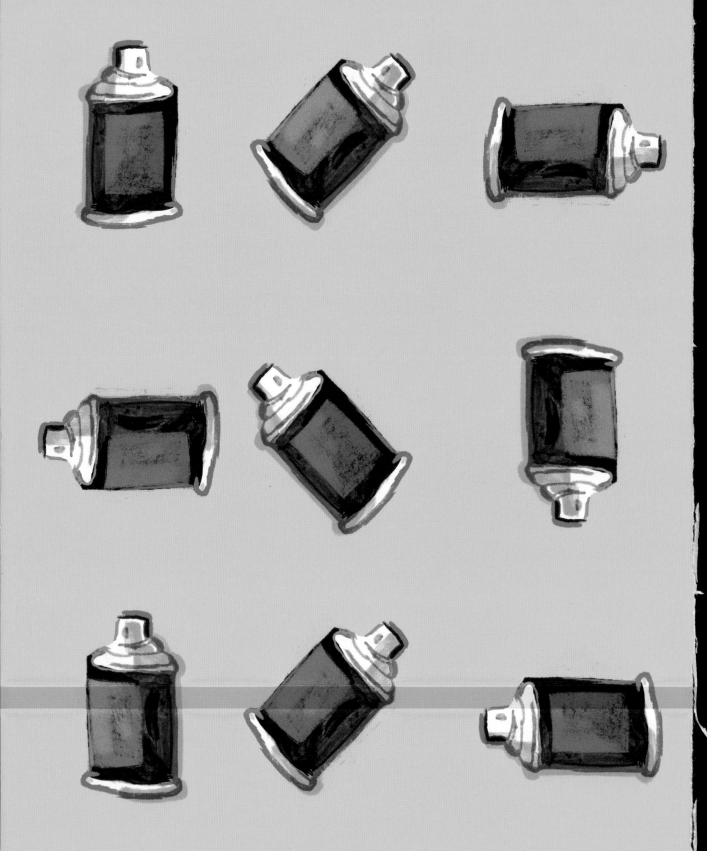